GNU Emacs
Pocket Reference

Debra Cameron

D1052220

O'REILLY®

Beijing • Cambridge • Farnham • Köln • Paris • Sebastopol • Taipei • Tokyo

GNU Emacs Pocket Reference

by Debra Cameron

Copyright © 1999 O'Reilly & Associates, Inc. All rights reserved.
Printed in the United States of America.

Editor: Gigi Estabrook

Production Editor: Claire Cloutier LeBlanc

Production Services: Omegatype Typography, Inc.

Cover Design: Edie Freedman

Printing History:

January 1999:   First Edition

Nutshell Handbook, the Nutshell Handbook logo, and the
O'Reilly logo are registered trademarks of O'Reilly & Associates,
Inc. The association between the image of a gnu and the topic
of GNU Emacs is a trademark of O'Reilly & Associates, Inc.

Many of the designations used by manufacturers and sellers to
distinguish their products are claimed as trademarks. Where
those designations appear in this book, and O'Reilly &
Associates, Inc. was aware of a trademark claim, the
designations have been printed in caps or initial caps. While
every precaution has been taken in the preparation of this book,
the publisher assumes no responsibility for errors or omissions,
or for damages resulting from the use of the information
contained herein.

This book is printed on acid-free paper with 85% recycled
content, 15% post-consumer waste. O'Reilly & Associates is
committed to using paper with the highest recycled content
available consistent with high quality.

ISBN: 1-56592-496-7   [11/99]

Table of Contents

GNU Emacs
Pocket Reference

Introduction

Emacs is a powerful text editor and, unlike most editors, it is a complete working environment. GNU Emacs is the most popular and widespread of the Emacs family of editors. Covering GNU Emacs 20.2, this small book has condensed Emacs reference material and provides a resource for readers of O'Reilly & Associates' *Learning GNU Emacs,* by Debra Cameron, Bill Rosenblatt, and Eric Raymond.

Emacs Commands

Emacs commands consist of a modifier, such as **CTRL** (CONTROL) or **ESC** (ESCAPE), followed by one or two characters. Commands shown in this book abbreviate **CTRL** to **C**:

C-g
    Hold down the **CTRL** key and press **g**.

Most Emacs manuals refer to the **META** key in addition to the **CTRL** key. Since most keyboards don't have a **META** key, this book refers to **ESC** instead of **META**:

ESC x
    Press **ESC**, release it, then press **x**.

It is entirely possible that your keyboard has a **META** key. On many keyboards, the **ALT** keys function as the **META** key. If your keyboard does have a **META** key, it works like the **CTRL** key described here—that is, you hold down the **META** key and press the desired key, such as **g**.

Conventions

UNIX commands, Emacs keystrokes, command names, menu options, and variables are shown in **boldface** type.

Filenames are shown in *italic* type.

Buffer names, LISP code, C code, Emacs messages, and other excerpts from programs are shown in `constant width` type.

Dummy parameters that you replace with an actual value are shown in *italic* type. (If they appear within code, they are shown in `constant width italic` type.)

1. Emacs Basics

A Word About Modes

Emacs achieves some of its famed versatility by having various editing modes in which it behaves slightly differently. The word *mode* may sound technical or complicated, but what it really means is that Emacs becomes sensitive to the task at hand.

Text mode and C mode are *major modes*. A buffer can be in only one major mode at a time; to exit a major mode, you have to enter another one.

Major modes

Whenever you edit a file, Emacs attempts to put you into the correct major mode. If you edit a file that ends in *.c,* it puts you into C mode. If you edit a file that ends in *.el,* it puts you in LISP mode.

Major Mode	Function
Fundamental mode	The default mode; no special behavior
Text mode	For writing text
Mail mode	For writing mail messages

Major Mode	Function
RMAIL mode	For reading and organizing mail
View mode	For viewing files but not editing
Shell mode	For running a UNIX shell within Emacs
Telnet mode	For logging in to remote systems
Outline mode	For writing outlines
Indented text mode	For indenting text automatically
Nroff mode	For formatting files for nroff
TEX mode	For formatting files for TEX
LATEX mode	For formatting files for LATEX
C mode	For writing C programs
C++ mode	For writing C++ programs
Java mode	For writing Java programs
FORTRAN mode	For writing FORTRAN programs
Emacs LISP mode	For writing Emacs LISP functions
LISP mode	For writing LISP programs
LISP interaction mode	For writing and evaluating LISP expressions

Minor modes

In addition to major modes, there are also *minor modes*. These define a particular aspect of Emacs behavior and can be turned on and off within a major mode.

Minor Mode	Function
Auto-fill mode	Enables word wrap
Overwrite mode	Replaces characters as you type instead of inserting them
Auto-save mode	Saves your file automatically every so often in an auto-save file

Minor Mode	Function
Abbrev mode	Allows you to define word abbreviations
Transient mark mode	Highlights selected regions of text
Outline mode	For writing outlines
VC mode	For using various version control systems under Emacs

Starting and Leaving Emacs

To	Keystrokes Command Name
Start Emacs	**emacs**
Edit a specific file in Emacs	**emacs** *filename*
Exit Emacs	**C-x C-c** **save-buffers-kill-emacs**
Suspend Emacs temporarily	**C-z** **suspend-emacs**

Working with Files

To	Keystrokes Command Name
Open a file	**C-x C-f** **find-file**
Open a different file instead	**C-x C-v** **find-alternate-file**
Insert file at cursor position	**C-x i** **insert-file**
Save a file	**C-x C-s** **save-buffer**
Save a file under another name	**C-x C-w** **write-file**
Create a new buffer	**C-x b** *buffername* **switch-to-buffer**

To	Keystrokes Command Name
Move to an existing buffer	**C-x b** *buffername* switch-to-buffer
Display the buffer list	**C-x C-b** list-buffers

Letting Emacs Fill in the Blanks

Emacs has a very helpful feature known as *completion*. If you open an existing file, type only the first few letters of the name, enough to make a unique filename. Press **TAB**, and Emacs completes the filename for you. Completion also works for long command names.

2. Editing Files

Working in Text Mode

Text mode is the standard mode for typing text. By default, Emacs does not do word wrap, instead creating very long lines. To enable word wrap, type **ESC x auto-fill-mode RETURN**.

You may decide that you want to enter auto-fill mode automatically whenever you edit. If so, add this line to the Emacs startup file, *.emacs,* which is located in your home directory. (If the startup file doesn't exist, create it.)

```
(setq default-major-mode 'text-mode)
(add-hook 'text-mode-hook 'turn-on-auto-fill)
```

Moving the Cursor

To move	Keystrokes Command Name
Forward one character	**C-f** forward-char
Backward one character	**C-b** backward-char

To move	Keystrokes Command Name
Up one line	C-p previous-line
Down one line (at the end of a file, creates a newline)	C-n next-line
Forward one word	ESC f forward-word
Backward one word	ESC b backward-word
To the beginning of the line	C-a beginning-of-line
To the end of the line	C-e end-of-line
Forward one screen	C-v scroll-up
Backward one screen	ESC v scroll-down
To the beginning of the file	ESC < beginning-of-buffer
To the end of the file	ESC > end-of-buffer

Repeating Commands

To	Keystrokes Command Name
Repeat the following command *n* times	ESC *n* digit-argument
Repeat the following command 4 times	C-u universal-argument
Repeat the following command 16 times	C-u C-u universal-argument

To	Keystrokes Command Name
Repeat a complex command (can edit arguments)	C-x ESC ESC repeat-complex-command
Recall previous command in minibuffer	ESC p previous-history-element

Cutting Text

Emacs has two distinct concepts when it comes to cutting text. You can delete text, which implies that you want to eliminate it entirely. Or you can kill text, which implies that you want to paste it in another location. Emacs stores killed text in the *kill ring*. Commands that use the word *kill* (such as **kill-word**) store text in the kill ring. Commands that use the word *delete* (such as **delete-char**) do not store the text in the kill ring.

To delete	Keystrokes Command Name
Character	C-d delete-char
Previous character	DEL delete-backward-char
Word	ESC d kill-word
Previous word	ESC DEL backward-kill-word
Line	C-k kill-line

Marking Text to Delete, Move, or Copy

In Emacs, you mark *regions* of text, which you can then delete, move, or copy. A region is the area between the point (the cursor) and the mark (which you set).

To	Keystrokes Command Name
Set the mark (beginning or end of a region)	C-@ *or* C-SPACE set-mark-command
Delete marked text	C-w kill-region
Copy a region	ESC w *or* C-Insert kill-ring-save
Paste a region	C-y *or* S-Insert yank
Paste an earlier deletion	ESC y yank-pop
Exchange location of point and mark	C-x C-x exchange-point-and-mark

Using a Mouse with Emacs

To	Keystrokes Command Name
Move cursor to where arrow is	Left mouse button mouse-set-point
Paste text	Middle mouse button x-paste-text
Copy region to the kill ring	Right mouse button x-cut-text
Cut region	C-middle button x-cut-and-wipe-text
Split window vertically	C-right button x-mouse-select-and-split
Copy region to the kill ring	S-middle button x-cut-text
Paste text	S-right x-paste-text
Delete all other windows but this one	C-S-right button x-mouse-keep-one- window

Transposing and Capitalizing Text

To	Keystrokes Command Name
Transpose two letters	C-t transpose-chars
Transpose two words	ESC t transpose-words
Transpose two lines	C-x C-t transpose-lines
Capitalize word	ESC c capitalize-word
Uppercase word	ESC u upcase-word
Lowercase word	ESC l downcase-word

Stopping Commands

When you want to stop any command that's in progress, press **C-g**. The word Quit appears in the command area.

Undoing Edits

What happens if you make a mistake while you're editing? You can undo your changes by pressing **C-x u**.

What if you'd like to redo a command after you type **undo**? There is no formal redo command, but you can use **undo** in the following way. Move the cursor in any direction, and type **C-x u** again. Emacs redoes the last command. You can repeat it to redo previous undos.

Although **undo** is an important command, it can be slow if you want to undo a large number of changes. The following table summarizes three methods for undoing changes and the circumstances for their use.

If you	Use this command
Don't like the recent changes you've made and want to undo them one by one	C-x u
Want to undo all changes made since the file was last saved	**ESC x revert-buffer RETURN**
Want to go back to an earlier version of the file (the file as it was when you started this editing session)	**C-x C-f** *filename~* **RETURN** **C-x C-w** *filename* **RETURN**

Recovering Lost Changes

Emacs saves your file every so often in an *auto-save* file. Using auto-save files, you can recover most, if not all, lost changes. Auto-save files use the current filename (text) but add a sharp (#) at the beginning and the end (#text#).

To recover text from an auto-save file, type **ESC x recover-file RETURN**. Emacs opens a window that lists both the file and its associated auto-save file so that you can compare the time at which they were created, their size, and so forth. Emacs asks you the following question:

```
Recover auto-save file #text#? (yes or no)
```

Emacs creates an auto-save file every few hundred keystrokes and any time the power is interrupted or Emacs is terminated abnormally.

If you were editing several files at once, try **ESC x recover-session RETURN** instead.

3. Search and Replace Operations

Incremental Search

An incremental search begins when you type the first letter and continues searching as you add characters.

To	Keystrokes Command Name
Incremental search forward	**C-s** isearch-forward
Incremental search backward	**C-r** isearch-backward
Exit incremental search	**RETURN**
Cancel incremental search	**C-g** keyboard-quit
Delete incorrect character of search string	**DEL**

Nonincremental and Word Search

Emacs provides a plain vanilla search, in which you type the whole word, then start the search. It also offers a word search. This search finds whole words and can find phrases spread across line breaks.

To	Keystrokes
Search forward	**C-s RETURN**
Search backward	**C-r RETURN**
Word search	**C-s RETURN C-w**

Query Replace

To	Keystrokes Command Name
Enter query-replace	**ESC %** query-replace
Replace and go on to the next instance	**SPACE** *or* **y**
Don't replace; move on to next instance	**DEL** *or* **n**
Replace the current instance and quit	**.**
Replace and pause (**SPACE** *or* **y** to move on)	**,**

To	Keystrokes Command Name
Replace the rest and don't ask	!
Back up to the previous instance	^
Exit query-replace	**RETURN** *or* q
Enter recursive edit	**C-r**
Delete this instance and enter a recursive edit	**C-w**
Exit recursive edit and resume query-replace	**ESC C-c**
Exit recursive edit and exit query-replace	**C-]**

Regular Expression Search and Replace

This section lists characters for creating regular expressions, followed by commands for replacement operations using regular expressions.

Characters for creating regular expressions

Symbol	Matches
^	The beginning of a line
$	The end of a line
.	Any single character (like ? in filenames)
.*	Any group of zero or more characters (like * in filenames)
\<	The beginning of a word
\>	The end of a word
[ ]	Any character specified within the brackets; for example, [a-z] matches any alphabetic character

Regular Expression Search Commands

To	Keystrokes Command Name
Search for a regular expression forward	ESC C-s RETURN re-search-forward
Search for a regular expression backward	ESC C-r RETURN re-search-backward
Search incrementally forward for a regular expression	ESC C-s isearch-forward-regexp
Repeat incremental regular expression search	C-s isearch-forward
Search incrementally backward for a regular expression	ESC C-r isearch-backward-regexp
Query-replace a regular expression	ESC x query-replace-regexp
Globally replace a regular expression unconditionally (use with caution)	ESC x replace-regexp

Spellchecking

To	Keystrokes Command Name
Spellcheck current word	ESC $ ispell-word
Spellcheck region	ESC x ispell-region
Spellcheck buffer	ESC x ispell-buffer
Spellcheck body of mail message	ESC x ispell-message
Pause spellcheck	C-g
Resume spellcheck	ESC x ispell-continue
Kill the spellcheck process	ESC x ispell-kill-ispell
List possible completions for current word (text mode)	ESC TAB ispell-complete-word

Word Abbreviations

Abbreviations can be used as shortcuts for long words or defined as the correct spelling for commonly misspelled words.

Global abbreviations work in every major mode; local abbreviations work only in the mode in which they were defined. To define abbreviations, you must first enter word abbreviation mode.

To	Keystrokes Command Name
Enter (or exit) word abbreviation mode	ESC x abbrev-mode
Define a global abbreviation	C-x a - *or* C-x a i g inverse-add-global-abbrev
Define a local (mode-specific) abbreviation	C-x a i l inverse-add-mode-abbrev
Undo the last word abbreviation	ESC x unexpand-abbrev
Write the word abbreviation file	ESC x write-abbrev-file
Edit word abbreviations	ESC x edit-abbrevs
View word abbreviations	ESC x list-abbrevs
Kill abbreviations for this session	ESC x kill-all-abbrevs

To add word abbreviations to your startup, insert these lines in your *.emacs* file:

```
(setq-default abbrev-mode t)
(read-abbrev-file "~/.abbrev_defs")
(setq save-abbrevs t)
```

After making these modifications, restart Emacs and define an abbreviation. Ignore the error message that appears. During this first session, you will need to issue the following command: **ESC x write-abbrev-file RETURN~/.abbrev_defs RETURN**. After this initial session, this file will be loaded and saved automatically.

4. Using Buffers and Windows

Using Buffers

To	Keystrokes Command Name
Move to the buffer specified	**C-x b** *buffername* **switch-to-buffer**
Display the buffer list	**C-x C-b** **list-buffers**
Delete the buffer specified	**C-x k** *buffername* **kill-buffer**
Ask about deleting each buffer	**ESC x kill-some-buffers**
Change the buffer's name	**ESC x rename-buffer**
Ask about saving each modified buffer	**C-x s** **save-some-buffers**

Buffer list commands

To	Keystrokes
Move to the next buffer	**SPACE** *or* n
Move to the previous buffer	p
Mark buffer for deletion	d *or* k
Save buffer	s
Unmark buffer	u
Execute other one-letter commands on all marked buffers	x
Unmark the previous buffer in the list	**DEL**
Mark buffer as unmodified	~
Toggle read-only status of buffer	%
Display buffer in a full screen	1

To	Keystrokes
Display this buffer and the next one in horizontal windows	2
Replace buffer list with this buffer	f
Replace other window with this buffer	o
Mark buffers to be displayed in windows	m
Display buffers marked with m; Emacs makes as many windows as needed	v
Quit buffer list	q

Using Windows

Windows subdivide the current Emacs window. To create new Emacs windows, see the following section on Frames.

To	Keystrokes / Command Name
Create two windows, one on top of the other	C-x 2 split-window-vertically
Move to the other window	C-x o other-window
Delete the current window	C-x 0 delete-window
Delete all windows but this one	C-x 1 delete-other-windows
Make window taller	C-x ^ enlarge-window
Make window shorter	ESC x shrink-window
Scroll other window	ESC C-v scroll-other-window
Find a file in another other window	C-x 4 f find-file-other-window
Delete buffer and window (asks for confirmation)	C-x 4 0 kill-buffer-and-window

Using Frames

Frame commands apply only when Emacs is running under a GUI, such as X Windows.

To	Keystrokes / Command Name
Make a new frame	C-x 5 2 make-frame-command
Move to another frame	C-x 5 o other-frame
Delete current frame	C-x 5 0 delete-frame
Find file in a new frame	C-x 5 f find-file-other-frame
Make frame and display other buffer in it	C-x 5 b switch-to-buffer-other-frame

Using Bookmarks

Bookmarks provide an easy way to get back to a particular place in a file. They are also handy shortcuts for quickly finding files with long pathnames.

Bookmark commands

To	Keystrokes / Command Name
Set a bookmark at the current cursor position	C-x r m bookmark-set
Jump to a bookmark	C-x r b bookmark-jump
Rename a bookmark	ESC x bookmark-rename
Delete a bookmark	ESC x bookmark-delete
Save bookmarks	ESC x bookmark-save
Move to bookmark list	C-x r l bookmark-bmenu-list

To	Keystrokes Command Name
Insert full text of file associated with a given bookmark	ESC x bookmark-insert
Save all bookmarks in a specified file	ESC x bookmark-write
Load bookmarks from a specified file	ESC x bookmark-load

Bookmark list

To	Keystrokes
Flag bookmark for deletion	d
Rename bookmark	r
Save all bookmarks listed	s
Display the bookmark the cursor is on	f
Mark bookmarks to be displayed in multiple windows	m
Display marked bookmarks or the one the cursor is on if none is marked	v
Toggle display of paths to files associated with bookmarks	t
Display location of file associated with bookmark	w
Delete bookmarks flagged for deletion	x
Remove mark from bookmark	u
Remove mark from bookmark on previous line	DEL
Exit bookmark list	q

5. Emacs as a Work Environment

Shell Mode

Shell mode lets you access the UNIX shell without leaving Emacs. A rule of thumb in shell mode is that you preface all ordinary control sequences with **C-c**. For example, to interrupt a command, type **C-c C-c**.

To	Keystrokes Command Name
Enter shell mode	**ESC x shell**
Interrupt current job; equivalent to **C-c** in UNIX shells	**C-c C-c** comint-interrupt-subjob
Delete a character; if at end of buffer send an EOF character	**C-d** comint-delchar-or-maybe-eof
Send EOF character	**C-c C-d** comint-send-eof
Erase current line; **C-u** in UNIX shells	**C-c C-u** comint-kill-input
Suspend or stop a job; **C-z** in UNIX shells	**C-c C-z** comint-stop-subjob
Display previous command; repeat to display earlier commands	**ESC p** comint-previous-input
Display subsequent commands; repeat to display more recent commands	**ESC n** comint-next-input
Execute command on current line	**RETURN** comint-send-input
Complete command, filename, or variable name	**TAB** comint-dynamic-complete

To	Keystrokes Command Name
Delete output from last command	C-c C-o comint-kill-output
Move last line of output to bottom of window	C-c C-e comint-show-maximum-output

Working with Dired

Dired is Emacs's directory editor. It provides a convenient way to manage files and directories.

To	Keystrokes Command Name
Start Dired	C-x d dired
Copy	C dired-do-copy
Flag for deletion	d dired-flag-file-deletion
Delete immediately	D dired-do-delete
Open file or directory	e or f dired-find-file
Reread the directory from disk	g revert-buffer
Change group permissions	G dired-do-chgrp
Remove line from display (don't delete it)	k dired-do-kill-lines
Mark with *	m dired-mark
Move to the next line	n dired-next-line
Find file in another window; move there	o dired-find-file-other-window

To	Keystrokes Command Name
Find file in another window; don't move there	C-o dired-display-file
Print file	P dired-do-print
Quit Dired	q dired-quit
Query-replace string in marked files	Q dired-do-query-replace
Rename file	R dired-do-rename
Unmark file	u dired-unmark
View file	v dired-view-file
Delete files flagged with D	x dired-do-flagged-delete
Compress file	Z dired-do-compress
Unmark all files (no matter what the mark was)	ESC DEL dired-unmark-all-files
Flag backup files for deletion; C-u ~ removes flags	~ dired-flag-backup-files
Flag auto-save files for deletion; C-u # removes flags	# dired-flag-auto-save-files
Flag numbered backups for deletion	. dired-clean-directory
Mark directories with *; C-u * / unmarks	* / dired-mark-directories
Compare this file to the file at the mark	= dired-diff
Compare this file with its backup file	ESC = dired-backup-diff
Execute shell command on this file	! dired-do-shell-command
Move to the next file marked with * or D	ESC } dired-next-marked-file

To	Keystrokes Command Name
Move to previous file marked with * or **D**	ESC { dired-prev-marked-file
Flag for deletion files that match regular expression	% d dired-flag-files-regexp
Mark files that match regular expression	% m dired-mark-files-regexp
Create a directory	+ dired-create-directory
Move to next directory	> dired-next-dirline
Move to previous directory	< dired-prev-dirline
Sort the Dired display by date or filename (toggles between these)	s dired-sort-toggle-or-edit

Printing

To	Keystrokes Command Name
Print buffer (similar to UNIX **pr | lpr**)	ESC x print-buffer
Print the region (similar to UNIX **pr | lpr**)	ESC x print-region
Print buffer with no page numbers (similar to UNIX lpr)	ESC x lpr-buffer
Print region with no page numbers (similar to UNIX lpr)	ESC x lpr-region
From Dired, insert the default print command in the minibuffer	p
Print the buffer with formatting intact	ESC x ps-print-buffer-with-faces

Calendar and Diary Commands

To	Keystrokes Command Name
Display the day of the year	**p d** calendar-print-day-of-year
Scroll the other window	**SPACE** scroll-other-window
Quit calendar	**q** exit-calendar
Add a weekly entry based on the day of the week	**i w** insert-weekly-diary-entry
Add an annual entry	**i y** insert-yearly-diary-entry
Add an entry for a particular day	**i d** insert-diary-entry
Add an entry for the day of the month	**i m** insert-monthly-diary-entry
Add an entry to recur every *n* days	**i c** insert-cyclic-diary-entry
Add a block entry	**i b** insert-block-diary-entry
Display diary entries in a different typeface, color, or marked with a plus sign	**m** mark-diary-entries
Display diary file	**s** show-all-diary-entries
Mark regions by time rather than horizontally	**C-SPACE** *or* **C-@** calendar-set-mark

6. Email and Newsgroups

Sending Mail

To	Keystrokes
Compose a mail message	C-x m
Compose a mail message in another window	C-x 4 m
Compose a mail message in another frame	C-x 5 m
Insert contents of the *.signature* file	C-c C-w
Send message	C-c C-c
Define an alias for a name or a group of names	ESC x define-mail-alias

Reading Mail with RMAIL

Emacs interfaces with a number of mail programs, but its own mail program is RMAIL.

To	Keystrokes
Read mail with RMAIL	ESC x rmail
Scroll to the next screen of the message	SPACE
Scroll to the previous screen of this message	DEL
Move to the beginning of this message	.
Move to the next message	n
Move to the previous message	p
Move to the first message	<
Move to the last message	>
Jump to a certain message (preface with the number of the message to jump to)	j

To	Keystrokes
Flag this message for deletion and move forward	d
Flag this message for deletion and move backward	C-d
Undelete a message that has been flagged for deletion	u
Delete all messages flagged for deletion	x
Save message in RMAIL file format	o *filename* RETURN
Save message as a standard ASCII text file	C-o *filename* RETURN
Display a window that lists all messages	h
Exit RMAIL	q

Reading Mail with Gnus

Emacs has a built-in newsreader called Gnus. To enter Gnus, type **ESC x gnus**. You'll see a group buffer, commands for which are listed below. Select the newsgroup you want to read. Commands for the summary buffer, which lists messages in a given newsgroup, are listed below as well.

Gnus group buffer commands

To	Keystrokes
Start Gnus	**ESC x gnus**
Read articles in the group the cursor is on	**SPACE**
Subscribe or unsubscribe to this group	u
Prompt for a group to jump to	j
List all newsgroups you subscribe to	l
List groups that have been killed (killed groups are listed in the *.newsrc.eld* file)	A k

To	Keystrokes
List all newsgroups available on this server	L
Get new news	g
Write a message for this group	a
Exit news and update *.newsrc* file	q

Gnus summary buffer commands

To	Keystrokes
Scroll forward	**SPACE**
Scroll backward	**DEL**
Move to the last posting you read	l
Get the FAQ for this newsgroup	H f
Move to the next article	n
Move to the previous article	p
Save article and mark with an exclamation point	u
Save the current article in UNIX format	C-o
Save the current article in RMAIL format	o
Go back to the Group buffer	q
Mark articles as read, starting with the current line and forward	d
Mail a copy of this article to someone	C-c C-f
Display current article	g
Delete all articles marked as read	x
Expand the Summary window	=

Gnus posting commands

To	Keystrokes
Post a new article	a
Reply to the person who posted the article	r

To	Keystrokes
Reply to the person who posted the article and include a copy of the article	R
Post a follow-up to the current article to Usenet	f
Post a follow-up to the current article to Usenet and include a copy of the original article	F
From the News buffer, insert the original article	C-c C-y
From the News buffer, fill yanked article (to create even line lengths)	C-c C-q
Post or mail the article	C-c C-c
From the Summary buffer, cancel a posting	C

7. Emacs and the Internet

Telnet Commands

To	Keystrokes Command Name
Start Telnet mode	ESC x telnet
Depending on the context, send EOF or delete the character under the cursor	C-d comint-delchar-or-maybe-eof
Process Telnet input	RETURN telnet-send-input
Interrupt current job; **C-c** in UNIX shells	C-c C-c telnet-interrupt-subjob
Send the next character quoted; similar to **C-q**	C-c C-q send-process-next-char
Send EOF character	C-c C-d comint-send-eof
Move first line of output to top of window	C-c C-r comint-show-output

To	Keystrokes Command Name
Move last line of output to bottom of window	C-c C-e comint-show-maximum-output
Delete output from last command	C-c C-o comint-kill-output
Suspend or stop a job; C-z in UNIX shells	C-c C-z telnet-c-z
Erase current line; C-u in UNIX shells	C-c C-u comint-kill-input
Retrieve subsequent commands (can be repeated to find more recent commands)	ESC n comint-next-input
Retrieve previous commands (can be repeated to find earlier commands)	ESC p comint-previous-input

Copying Files with Ange-ftp Mode

Ange-ftp mode alleviates the need for learning FTP commands. Essentially, you "find" files on remote systems using C-x C-f, then copy them using Dired commands (described in Section 5). Ange-ftp mode is a transparent interface to FTP that is included in Emacs.

Emacs starts ange-ftp mode if the following three conditions are met:

1. The filename begins with a slash (/).

2. The slash is followed by *username@systemname*.

3. There is a colon (:) between the system name and the directory or filenames, if any (for example, */anonymous@rtfm.mit.ed u:/pub*).

For example, typing */anonymous@rtfm.mit.edu:/pub* opens an FTP connection to rtfm.mit.edu and displays the */pub* directory. Don't forget the slash at the beginning or the colon between the system name and the path to the file.

Using the Web with Emacs

Emacs includes commands for invoking web browsers. The default browser is set to Netscape, but can be changed by setting the variable **browse-url-browser-function**.

Alternatively, you can download and install a web browser that works from within Emacs, W3 mode, available at *ftp://cs.indiana.edu/pub/elisp/w3/w3.tar.gz*.

To	Keystrokes Command Name
Start the default browser	**ESC x browse-url**
Browse the URL at the cursor position	**ESC x browse-url-at-point**
Browse the URL at the mouse location	**ESC x browse-url-at-mouse**

8. Simple Text Formatting and Specialized Editing

Centering Commands

Centering commands work only in text mode.

To	Keystrokes Command Name
Center a line	**ESC s** center-line
Center a paragraph	**ESC S** center-paragraph
Center a region	**ESC x center-region**

Inserting Page Breaks
and Control Characters

To insert a page break in a file, type **C-q C-l**. **C-q** is the
quoted-insert command; it inserts the next control sequence
as a control character rather than interpreting it as an Emacs
command. You can also search and replace control characters by prefacing the search string with **C-q** in query-replace.

Rectangle Editing

Rectangle editing is particularly useful for deleting or rear-
ranging columns of data.

To	Keystrokes Command Name
Delete a rectangle and store it	**C-x r k** kill-rectangle
Delete a rectangle; do not store it	**C-x r d** delete-rectangle
Insert the last rectangle killed	**C-x r y** yank-rectangle
Blank out the area marked as a rectangle; do not store it	**C-x r c** clear-rectangle
Insert a blank rectangle in the area marked	**C-x r o** open-rectangle

Outline Mode Commands

To	Keystrokes Command Name
Move to the next heading	**C-c C-n** outline-next-visible- heading
Move to the previous heading	**C-c C-p** outline-previous- visible-heading

To	Keystrokes Command Name
Move to the next heading of the same level	C-c C-f outline-forward-same-level
Move to the previous heading of the same level	C-c C-b outline-backward-same-level
Move up one heading level	C-c C-u outline-up-heading
Hide all body lines	C-c C-t hide-body
Hide subheads and bodies associated with a given heading	C-c C-d hide-subtree
Hide the body associated with a particular heading (not subheads and their bodies)	ESC x hide-entry
Hide the body of a particular heading and the bodies of all its subheads	C-c C-l hide-leaves
Show everything that's hidden	C-c C-a show-all

9. Marking Up Text with Emacs

nroff Mode

To	Keystrokes Command Name
Enter nroff mode	ESC x nroff-mode
Move the cursor to the next text line	ESC n forward-text-line
Move the cursor to the previous text line	ESC p backward-text-line

To	Keystrokes Command Name
Enter electric nroff mode (a minor mode in which you type the first in a pair of nroff commands, then press C-j, and Emacs inserts the second command of the pair)	ESC x electric-nroff-mode
Complete common macro pairs	C-j electric-nroff-newline

TeX Mode

To	Keystrokes Command Name
Enter TeX mode	ESC x plain-tex-mode
Enter LaTeX mode	ESC x latex-mode
Insert two hard returns (standard end of paragraph) and check syntax of paragraph	C-j tex-terminate-paragraph
Insert two braces and put cursor between them	C-c { tex-insert-braces
Position the cursor following the closing brace, if you are between braces	C-c } up-list
Check buffer for syntax errors	ESC x validate-tex-buffer
Process buffer in TeX or LaTeX	C-c C-b tex-buffer
Put the message shell on the screen, showing (at least) the last error message	C-c C-l tex-recenter-output-buffer
Process region in TeX or LaTeX	C-c C-r tex-region
Kill TeX or LaTeX processing	C-c C-k tex-kill-job

To	Keystrokes Command Name
Print TEX or LATEX output	C-c C-p tex-print
Show print queue	C-c C-q tex-show-print-queue
Provide closing element of a command pair, in LATEX mode only	C-c C-e tex-close-latex-block

Html-Helper Mode

Html-helper mode by Nelson Minar offers great flexibility in writing HTML, with hand-holding features that you can turn on or off, depending on your level of expertise and preferences. We prefer it to Emacs's own html mode.

Html-helper mode is not part of Emacs by default. It is available at *ftp://ftp.reed.edu/pub/src/html-helper-mode.tar.gz*.

Once you get this file, put it in a directory such as *~/elisp*, move to that directory, and then type:

```
% gunzip html-helper-mode.tar.gz
% tar xvf html-helper-mode.tar
```

To make html-helper mode part of your startup, put the following lines in your *.emacs* file:

```
(setq load-path (cons "PUT_THE_PATH_HERE"
  load-path))
(autoload 'html-helper-mode "html-helper-mode"
  "Yay HTML" t)
(setq auto-mode-alist (cons '("\\.html$" .
  html-helper-mode)
auto-mode-alist))
```

To insert a skeleton in new HTML files, add this line:

```
(setq html-helper-build-new-buffer t)
```

To have html-helper mode prompt for input (such as URLs for hyperlinks), add this line:

```
(setq tempo-interactive t)
```

To insert and update timestamps every time you save an
HTML file, add this line:

```
(setq html-helper-do-write-file-hooks t)
```

Html-Helper Mode Commands

To	Keystrokes Command Name
Insert tags around a region, when used before a tag command	C-u universal-argument
Insert escape code for greater than sign, >	C-c > tempo-template-html-greater-than
Insert escape code for less than sign, <	C-c < tempo-template-html-less-than
Insert a paragraph delimiter, <p>	ESC RETURN tempo-template-html-paragraph
Insert <strong></strong>	C-c C-s s tempo-template-html-strong
Insert <em></em>	C-c C-s e tempo-template-html-emphasized
Insert <i></i>	C-c C-p i tempo-template-html-italic
Insert <b></b>	C-c C-p b tempo-template-html-bold
Insert <ul><li></ul>	C-c C-l u tempo-template-html-unordered-list

To	Keystrokes Command Name
Insert \<ol>\<li>\</ol>	C-c C-l o tempo-template-html-ordered-list
Insert \<dt>\<dd>	C-c C-l t tempo-template-html-definition-item
Insert \<li>	C-c C-l l tempo-template-html-item
Insert \<dl>\<dt> \<dd> \</dl>	C-c C-l d tempo-template-html-definition-list
Complete the current tag	ESC TAB tempo-complete-tag
Insert a literal line break, \ 	C-c RETURN tempo-template-html-break
Insert a horizontal rule, \<hr>	C-c - tempo-template-html-horizontal-rule
Insert timestamp delimiters	ESC C-t html-helper-insert-timestamp-delimiter-at-point
Insert \<title>\</title>	C-c C-b t tempo-template-html-title
Insert \<a href="">\</a>	C-c C-a l tempo-template-html-anchor
Insert \<a name="">\</a>	C-c C-a n tempo-template-html-target-anchor
Insert \<h1>\</h1>	C-c C-t 1 tempo-template-html-header-1

To	Keystrokes Command Name

Insert <h2></h2>	C-c C-t 2
	    tempo-template-html-
	    header-2

Insert <img align= ""
src="" alt="">
	C-c TAB e
	    tempo-template-html-
	    align-alt-image

Insert <img src="">	C-c TAB i
	    tempo-template-html-
	    image

Insert ,<img alt="" src="">	C-c TAB t
	    tempo-template-html-alt-
	    image

Insert <img align="" src="">	C-c TAB a
	    tempo-template-html-
	    align-image

10. Writing Macros

Macro Commands

To	Keystrokes Command Name
Start defining a macro	C-x (start-kbd-macro
End macro definition	C-x) end-kbd-macro
Execute last macro defined	C-x e call-last-kbd-macro

Execute the last macro
defined *n* times
	ESC *n* C-x e
	    digit-argument; call-last-
	    kbd-macro

Execute the last macro
defined and then add
keystrokes to it
	C-u C-x (
	    universal-argument;
	    start-kbd-macro

Name the last macro created (a preface to saving it)	ESC x name-last-kbd-macro

To	Keystrokes Command Name
Save a named macro in a file	ESC x insert-keyboard- macro
Load a named macro	ESC x load-file
Execute a named macro	ESC x *macroname*
Insert a query in a macro definition	C-x q kbd-macro-query

Insert a recursive edit in a
macro definition
	C-u C-x q
	   universal argument;
	   kbd-macro-query

Exit a recursive edit	ESC C-c exit-recursive-edit

11. Customizing Emacs

Keyboard Customization

You customize key bindings using one of three functions:
define-key, global-set-key, or local-set-key. Their forms are:

```
(define-key keymap "keystroke" 'command-name)
(global-set-key "keystroke" 'command-name)
(local-set-key "keystroke" 'command-name)
```

Notice the double quotes around keystroke and the single
quote preceding command-name. This is LISP syntax. The
"keystroke" is one or more characters, either printable or
special characters. Special characters, such as ESC, should be
represented as shown in the table below.

Special character conventions

Special Character	Definition
\C-*n*	C-*n* (where *n* is any letter)
\C-[*or* \e	ESC
\C-j *or* \n	LINEFEED

Special Character	Definition
\C-m *or* \r	RETURN
\C-i *or* \t	TAB

Emacs Variables

To set the value of a variable, use the setq function in your *.emacs* file, as in:

```
(setq auto-save-interval 800)
```

Although auto-save-interval takes an integer value, many Emacs variables take "true" or "false" values. In Emacs LISP, **t** is true and **nil** is false. Emacs variables can also take other types of values; here is how to specify them:

- Strings of characters are surrounded by double quotes.

- Characters are specified like strings but with a ? preceding them, and they are not surrounded by double quotes. Thus, ?x and ?\C-c are character values x and C-c, respectively.

- Symbols are specified by a single quote followed by a symbol name—for example, 'never.

A list of some useful Emacs variables with descriptions and default values follows.

Backups and auto-save

Variable Default	Description
make-backup-files t	If **t**, create a backup version of the current file before saving it for the first time.
backup-by-copying nil	If **t**, create backup files by copying rather than renaming the file. The default is renaming, which is more efficient.

Variable Default	Description
version-control nil	If t, create numbered versions of files as backups (with names of the form file-name~n~). If nil, only do this for files that have numbered versions already. If 'never, never make numbered versions.
kept-new-versions 2	Number of latest versions of a file to keep when a new numbered backup is made.
kept-old-versions 2	Number of oldest versions of a file to keep when a new numbered backup is made.
delete-old-versions nil	If t, delete excess versions without first asking for confirmation. If nil, ask for confirmation. If any other value, don't delete excess versions.
auto-save-default t	If t, auto-save every file visited.
auto-save-visited- file-name nil	If t, auto-save to the file being visited rather than to an auto-save file.
auto-save-interval 300	Number of keystrokes between auto-saving; if 0, turn off auto-saving.
auto-save-timeout 30	Seconds of inactivity after which Emacs auto-saves. If nil or 0, turn off this feature.

Variable Default	Description
delete-auto-save-files t	Non-nil means delete auto-save files whenever the "real" file is saved.
buffer-offer-save nil	Non-nil means offer to save the current buffer when exiting Emacs, even if the buffer is not a file.

Search and replace

Variable Default	Description
case-fold-search t	If non-nil, treat upper- and lowercase letters as the same when searching.
case-replace t	If non-nil, preserve the original case of letters when doing replaces (even if case-fold-search is on).
search-upper-case 'not-yanks	If non-nil, uppercase letters in search strings force search to be case-sensitive. The symbol 'not-yanks means convert uppercase letters in yanked text to lowercase.
search-exit-option t	If non-nil, any control character other than those defined in incremental search (**DEL, LINE-FEED, C-q, C-r, C-s, C-w, C-y**) exits search.
search-slow-speed 1200	If terminal is communicating at this speed or slower, use slow-style incremental search, in which a small window shows partial search results.

Variable Default	Description
search-highlight t	If non-nil, highlight partial search matches (GUI only).
query-replace-highlight nil	If non-nil, highlight matches in query-replace mode (GUI only).

Display

Variable Default	Description
next-screen-context-lines 2	Retain this many lines when scrolling forward or backward by **C-v** or **ESC-v**.
scroll-step 0	When moving the cursor vertically, scroll this many lines forward or backward.
scroll-step 0	When moving the cursor horizontally, scroll this many columns left or right.
tab-width 8	Width of tab stops; local to the current buffer.
truncate-lines nil	If non-nil, truncate long lines and use **$** to show that the line continues off-screen.
truncate-partial-width-windows t	If non-nil, truncate long lines (as above) in all windows that are not the full width of the display.
window-min-height 4	Minimum allowable height of windows (in lines).
window-min-width 10	Minimum allowable width of vertically split windows (in columns).

Variable Default	Description
split-window-keep-point t	When splitting windows, non-nil means keep point at same place in both new windows. If **nil**, choose new location of point to minimize redrawing (good for slow displays).
resize-minibuffer-mode nil	If non-nil, allow minibuffer to increase height to fit its contents.
resize-minibuffer- window-exactly t	Change size of minibuffer window dynamically so that it is exactly large enough to display its messages.
resize-minibuffer-frame nil	If non-nil, allow minibuffer frame (in GUI systems) to change height.
resize-minibuffer-frame- exactly t	Change size of the minibuffer frame (in GUI systems) dynamically so that it is exactly large enough to display its messages.
resize-minibuffer- window-max-height nil	Maximum size the minibuffer can grow to in resize-minibuffer-mode; in GUIs, if less than 1 or not a number, the limit is the height of the minibuffer frame.
ctl-arrow t	Non-nil means display control characters using ^X, where X is the letter being "controlled." Otherwise, use octal (base 8) ASCII notation for display—for example, C-h appears as \010 in octal.
display-time-day-and-date nil	If non-nil, **ESC x display-time RETURN** also shows day and date.

Variable Default	Description
line-number-mode t	If non-nil, display line number on mode line.
line-number-display-limit 1,000,000	Maximum size of buffer (in characters) for which line numbers should be displayed.
column-number-mode nil	If non-nil, display the column number on the mode line.
visible-bell nil	If non-nil, "flash" the screen instead of beeping when necessary.
track-eol nil	If non-nil, whenever the cursor is at the end of the line, "stick" to the end of the line when moving the cursor up or down; otherwise, stay in the column where the cursor is.
blink-matching-paren t	If non-nil, blink matching open parenthesis character when a closing parenthesis is typed.
blink-matching-paren-distance 25,600	Maximum number of characters to search through to find a matching open parenthesis character when a close parenthesis is typed.
blink-matching-delay 1	Number of seconds to pause when blinking a matching parenthesis.
echo-keystrokes 1	Echo prefixes for unfinished commands (e.g., **ESC-**) in minibuffer after user pauses for this many seconds; **0** means don't do echoing at all.
insert-default-directory t	If non-nil, insert the current directory in the minibuffer when asking for a filename.

Variable Default	Description
inverse-video nil	If non-nil, use reverse video for the entire display (normal video for mode lines).
mode-line-inverse-video t	Non-nil means use reverse video for mode lines.
highlight-nonselected- windows nil	If non-nil, highlight regions in windows other than the one currently selected (GUI only).
mouse-scroll-delay 0.25	Delay, in seconds, between screen scrolls when mouse is clicked and dragged from inside a window to beyond its borders. 0 means scroll as fast as possible.
mouse-scroll-min-lines 1	Scroll at least this many lines when mouse is dragged up or down beyond a window.

Modes

Variable Default	Description
major-mode fundamental-mode	Default mode for new buffers, unless set by virtue of the file-name; when setting this variable, precede the mode name with a single quote.
left-margin 0	Number of columns to indent when typing C-j in fundamental mode and text mode.
indent-tabs-mode t	If non-nil, allow the use of tab characters (as well as spaces) when indenting with C-j.
find-file-run-dired t	When visiting a file, run **dired** if the filename is a directory and this is non-nil.

Variable Default	Description
dired-kept-versions 2	When cleaning a directory in Dired, keep this many versions of files.
dired-listing-switches "-al"	Options passed to the **ls** command for generating Dired listings; should contain at least "-l".
$SHELL	Filename of shell to run with functions that use one, such as **list-directory**, **dired**, and **compile**; taken from value of the UNIX environment variable **SHELL**.
load-path	List of directories to search for LISP packages to load; often set to LISP subdirectory of directory where Emacs source code is installed.

Mail

Variable Default	Description
mail-self-blind nil	If non-nil, automatically insert your own name in the BCC (blind copy) field to ensure that you save a copy of your mail.
rmail-mail-new-frame nil	If non-nil, create a new frame for creating outgoing mail messages (GUI only).
mail-default-reply-to nil	Character string to insert in Reply-to: field of mail messages by default.

Variable Default	Description
mail-use-rfc822 nil	If non-nil, use the full RFC822 parser on mail addresses (takes longer but increases odds that complex addresses are parsed correctly).
mail-host-address nil	Name of your machine; can be used for constructing **user-mail-address**.
user-mail-address "*your email address*"	Your full email address.
rmail-primary-inbox-list nil	List of files containing incoming (unread) mail; if **nil**, use value of **$MAIL** environment variable, or, if that doesn't exist, use this path: /usr/spool/mail/*yourname*.
rmail-file-name "*~/RMAIL*"	File where RMAIL puts mail messages.
mail-archive-file-name nil	Character string used as name of the file to save all outgoing messages in; if **nil**, don't save all outgoing messages.
mail-personal-alias-file "*~/.mailrc*"	Name of the file in which to store mail aliases; RMAIL mail mode uses the same format for aliases as the standard UNIX **mail** and **mailx** programs.
mail-signature nil	Text to insert at end of outgoing mail messages.
rmail-dont-reply-to-names nil	Regular expression specifying names to omit when constructing lists of addresses to reply to; if **nil**, omit yourself from reply list.

Variable Default	Description
rmail-displayed-headers nil	Regular expression specifying which message header fields to display; if nil, display all headers except those included in **rmail-ignored-headers**.
rmail-ignored-headers	Regular expression specifying which message header fields not to display.
rmail-highlighted-headers "^From:\\\|^Subject:"	Regular expression specifying message headers to highlight (GUI only).
rmail-delete-after-output nil	If non-nil, automatically delete a message if it is saved in a file.
mail-from-style 'angles	Format of usernames in From: fields; if **nil**, include mail address only. If **'angles**, enclose mail address in angle brackets. If **'parens**, enclose it in parentheses.

Text editing

Variable Default	Description
sentence-end-double-space t	If non-nil, do not treat single spaces after periods as ends of sentences.
paragraph-separate "[\f]*$"	Regular expression that matches beginnings of lines that separate paragraphs.
paragraph-start "[\n\f]"	Regular expression that matches beginnings of lines that start or separate paragraphs.
page-delimiter "^\f"	Regular expression that matches page breaks.

Variable Default	Description
tex-default-mode 'plain-tex-mode	Mode to invoke when creating a file that could be either TEX or LATEX.
tex-run-command "tex"	Character string used as a command to run TEX in a subprocess on a file in TEX mode.
Latex-run-command "latex"	String used as a command to run LATEX in a subprocess.
slitex-run-command "slitex"	String used as a command to run SliTeX in a subprocess.
tex-dvi-print-command "lpr -d"	Character string used as a command to print a file in TEX mode with C-c C-p.
tex-dvi-view-command nil	Character string used as command to view a *.dvi* TEX output file with C-c C-v; usually set to *xdvi* on X Window systems.
tex-offer-save t	If non-nil, offer to save any unsaved buffers before running TEX.
tex-show-queue-command "lpq"	Character string used as command to show the print queue with C-c C-q in TEX mode.
tex-directory "."	Directory for TEX to put temporary files in; default is the current directory.
outline-regexp "[*\f]+"	Regular expression that matches heading lines in outline mode.
outline-heading-end-regexp "\n"	Regular expression that matches ends of heading lines in outline mode.
selective-display-ellipses t	If t, display "..." in place of hidden text in outline mode; otherwise, don't display anything.

Completion

Variable Default	Description
completion-auto-help t	If non-nil, provide help if a completion (via **TAB** or **RETURN** in minibuffer) is invalid or ambiguous.
completion-ignored-extensions	List of filename suffixes Emacs ignores when completing file-names.
completion-ignore-case nil	If non-nil, ignore case distinctions when doing completion.

Miscellaneous

Variable Default	Description
kill-ring-max 30	Keep *n* pieces of deleted text in the kill ring before deleting oldest kills.
require-final-newline nil	If a file being saved is missing a final **LINEFEED**, **nil** means don't add one, **t** means add one automatically, and other values mean ask for confirmation.
next-line-add-newlines t	If non-nil, **next-line** (**C-n** or down arrow) inserts newlines when at the end of the buffer, rather than signaling an error.

12. Emacs for Programmers

General Commands

Some of Emacs's commands are common to all supported programming languages.

To	Keystrokes Command Name
Indent each line between the cursor and mark	ESC C-\ indent-region
Move to the first nonblank character on the line	ESC m back-to-indentation
Join this line to the previous one	ESC ^ delete-indentation
Format and indent a comment	ESC ; indent-for-comment

C, C++, and Java Modes

To	Keystrokes Command Name
Move to the beginning of the current statement	ESC a c-beginning-of-statement
Move to the end of the current statement	ESC e c-end-of-statement
Fill the paragraph, preserving indentations and decorations, if in comment	ESC x c-fill-paragraph
Move to the beginning of current function	ESC C-a beginning-of-defun
Move to the end of current function	ESC C-e end-of-defun
Put the cursor at the beginning of function, mark at the end	C-c RETURN c-mark-function

To	Keystrokes Command Name
Indent the entire function according to indentation style	C-c C-q c-indent-defun
Indent a balanced expression according to indentation style	ESC C-q c-indent-exp
Toggle auto state, in which Emacs automatically indents or inserts newlines when "electric" characters are typed ({ } : # ; , / *)	C-c C-a c-toggle-auto-state
Toggle hungry state, in which Emacs deletes groups of spaces with a single DEL	C-c C-d c-toggle-hungry-state
Toggle auto-hungry state, in which Emacs deletes groups of spaces and the newline that precedes them with a single DEL	C-c C-t c-toggle-auto-hungry-state
Move to the beginning of the current preprocessor conditional	C-c C-u c-up-conditional
Move to the previous preprocessor conditional	C-c C-p c-backward-conditional
Move to the next preprocessor conditional	C-c C-n c-forward-conditional
Add and align backslashes at the end of each line in the region	C-c C-\ c-backslash-region
Comment the current region	C-c C-c comment-region

Customizing code indentation style

To select a code indentation style, type **C-c .** (for **c-set-style**). Possible styles are shown in the following table.

Style	Description
cc-mode	The default coding style, from which all others are derived
gnu	Style used in C code for Emacs itself and other GNU-related programs
k&r	Style of the classic text on C, Kernighan and Ritchie's *The C Programming Language*
bsd	Style used in code for BSD-derived versions of UNIX
stroustrup	C++ coding style of the standard reference work, Bjarne Stroustrup's *The C++ Programming Language*
whitesmith	Style used in Whitesmith Ltd.'s documentation for their C and C++ compilers
ellemtel	Style used in C++ documentation from Ellemtel Telecommunication Systems Laboratories in Sweden
linux	Style used by Linux developers
python	Style used by Python extension developers
java	Style used when writing Java code (entering Java mode selects this option by default)

LISP Mode

To	Keystrokes Command Name
Move backward by one S-expression	ESC C-b backward-sexp
Move forward by one S-expression	ESC C-f forward-sexp
Transpose the S-expressions around the cursor	ESC C-t transpose-sexps
Set mark at the end of the current S-expression, cursor at the beginning	ESC C-@ *or* ESC C-SPACE mark-sexp
Delete the S-expression following the cursor	ESC C-k kill-sexp
Delete the S-expression preceding the cursor	ESC C-DEL backward-kill-sexp
Move forward by one list	ESC C-n forward-list
Move backward by one list	ESC C-p backward-list
Move forward and down one parenthesis level	ESC C-d down-list
Move forward out of one parenthesis level	ESC x up-list
Move backward out of one parenthesis level	ESC C-u backward-up-list
Move to the beginning of the current function	ESC C-a beginning-of-defun
Move to the end of the current function	ESC C-e end-of-defun
Put cursor at beginning of function, mark at end	ESC C-h mark-defun

FORTRAN Mode

To	Keystrokes Command Name
Move forward one statement	C-c C-n fortran-next-statement
Move backward one statement	C-c C-p fortran-previous-statement
Move to the beginning of the current subprogram	ESC C-a beginning-of-fortran-subprogram
Move to the end of the current subprogram	ESC C-e end-of-fortran-subprogram
Put the cursor at beginning of subprogram, mark at end	ESC C-h mark-fortran-subprogram

13. Version Control Under Emacs

Version Control Commands

To	Keystrokes Command Name
Go to the next logical version control state	C-x v v vc-next-action
Show all registered files beneath a directory	C-x v d vc-directory
Generate a version difference report	C-x v = vc-diff
Throw away changes since the last checked-in revision	C-x v u vc-revert-buffer
Retrieve a given revision in another window	C-x v ~ vc-version-other-window
Display a file's change comments and history	C-x v l vc-print-log

To	Keystrokes Command Name
Register a file for version control	C-x v i vc-register
Insert version control headers in a file	C-x v h vc-insert-headers
Check out a named project snapshot	C-x v r vc-retrieve-snapshot
Create a named project snapshot	C-x v s vc-create-snapshot
Throw away a saved revision	C-x v c vc-cancel-version
Update a GNU-style ChangeLog file	C-x v a vc-update-change-log

Version Control Variables

Variable Default	Description
vc-default-back-end 'RCS	Version control system used with the VC package. Valid values are the symbols 'RCS, 'CVS, and 'SCCS.
vc-display-status t	If non-nil, display the version number and the locked state in the mode line.
vc-keep-workfiles t	If non-nil, do not delete workfiles after you register changes with the VC system.
vc-mistrust-permissions nil	If non-nil, do not assume that a file's owner ID and permission flags reflect version control system's idea of file's ownership and permission; get this information directly from VC system.
diff-switches -c	-c forces context-diff format; -u is unified-diff format.

Variable Default	Description
vc-make-backup-files nil	If non-nil, make standard Emacs backups of files registered with VC system.
vc-consult-headers t	If non-nil, determine version numbers by looking at headers in workfiles; otherwise, get this information from master file.

14. Online Help

The Help System

The help system commands answer certain questions. This table lists the questions and the commands used to ask them.

Question	Keystrokes Command Name
What command does this keystroke sequence run?	C-h c describe-key-briefly
What command does this keystroke sequence run, and what does it do?	C-h k describe-key
What were the last 100 characters I typed?	C-h l view-lossage
What is the key binding for this command?	C-h w where-is
What does this function do?	C-h f describe-function
What does this variable mean, and what is its value?	C-h v describe-variable
What mode is the current buffer in?	C-h m describe-mode
What are all the key bindings for this buffer?	C-h b describe-bindings

Question	Keystrokes Command Name
How do I run the Emacs tutorial?	C-h t help-with-tutorial
How do I start the **Info** documentation reader?	C-h i info

Apropos Commands

Apropos commands help you discover commands and variables related to a given concept or keyword. Apropos is useful for learning new things about Emacs.

Question Answered	Keystrokes Command Name
What commands involve this concept?	C-h a command-apropos
What functions and variables involve this concept?	ESC x apropos

Information About Emacs

To	Keystrokes Command Name
Run the Emacs tutorial	C-h t help-with-tutorial
Start the **Info** documentation reader	C-h i info
Start the **Info** documentation reader and go to the node for a given command	C-h C-f Info-goto-emacs-command-node
Start the **Info** documentation reader and go to the node for a given keystroke sequence	C-h C-k Info-goto-emacs-key-command-node
View news about recent changes in Emacs	C-h n view-emacs-news

To	Keystrokes Command Name
View a FAQ about Emacs	C-h F view-emacs-FAQ
Get information about Emacs LISP packages available on your system	C-h p finder-by-keyword
View the Emacs General Public License	C-h C-c describe-copying
View information on ordering Emacs from FSF	C-h C-d describe-distribution
View information on the GNU project	C-h C-p describe-project
View the (non-)warranty for Emacs	C-h C-w describe-no-warranty

More Titles from O'Reilly

UNIX Tools

lex & yacc, 2nd Edition

By John Levine, Tony Mason &
Doug Brown
2nd Edition October 1992
366 pages, ISBN 1-56592-000-7

sed & awk, 2nd Edition

By Dale Dougherty & Arnold Robbins
2nd Edition March 1997
432 pages, ISBN 1-56592-225-5

The UNIX CD Bookshelf

By O'Reilly & Associates, Inc.
1st Edition November 1998 (est.)
444 pages (est.)
Includes CD-ROM & book
ISBN 1-56592-406-1

Managing Projects with make, 2nd Edition

By Andrew Oram & Steve Talbott
2nd Edition October 1991
152 pages, ISBN 0-937175-90-0

UNIX Power Tools, 2nd Edition

By Jerry Peek, Tim O'Reilly &
Mike Loukides
2nd Edition August 1997
1120 pages, Includes CD-ROM
ISBN 1-56592-260-3

Writing GNU Emacs Extensions

By Bob Glickstein
1st Edition April 1997
236 pages, ISBN 1-56592-261-1

Exploring Expect

By Don Libes
1st Edition December 1994
602 pages, ISBN 1-56592-090-2

Programming with GNU Software

By Mike Loukides & Andy Oram
1st Edition December 1996
260 pages, ISBN 1-56592-112-7

Applying RCS and SCCS

By Don Bolinger & Tan Bronson
1st Edition September 1995
528 pages, ISBN 1-56592-117-8

Tcl/Tk Tools

By Mark Harrison
1st Edition September 1997
678 pages, Includes CD-ROM
ISBN 1-56592-218-2

O'REILLY

TO ORDER: **800-998-9938** • **order@oreilly.com** • **http://www.oreilly.com/**
OUR PRODUCTS ARE AVAILABLE AT A BOOKSTORE OR SOFTWARE STORE NEAR YOU.
FOR INFORMATION: **800-998-9938** • **707-829-0515** • **info@oreilly.com**

UNIX Tools

Software Portability with imake, 2nd Edition

By Paul DuBois
2nd Edition September 1996
410 pages, ISBN 1-56592-226-3

Tcl/Tk in a Nutshell

By Paul Raines & Jeff Tranter
1st Edition January 1999 (est.)
528 pages, ISBN 1-56592-433-9

C and C++

C++: The Core Language

By Gregory Satir & Doug Brown
1st Edition October 1995
228 pages, ISBN 1-56592-116-X

Practical C++ Programming

By Steve Oualline
1st Edition September 1995
584 pages, ISBN 1-56592-139-9

Checking C Programs with lint

By Ian F. Darwin
1st Edition October 1988
84 pages, ISBN 0-937175-30-7

Practical C Programming, 3rd Edition

By Steve Oualline
3rd Edition August 1997
454 pages, ISBN 1-56592-306-5

High Performance Computing, 2nd Edition

By Kevin Dowd & Charles Severance
2nd Edition July 1998
466 pages, ISBN 1-56592-312-X

UML in a Nutshell

By Sinan Si Alhir
1st Edition September 1998
290 pages, ISBN 1-56592-448-7

O'REILLY®

TO ORDER: **800-998-9938** • **order@oreilly.com** • **http://www.oreilly.com/**
OUR PRODUCTS ARE AVAILABLE AT A BOOKSTORE OR SOFTWARE STORE NEAR YOU.
FOR INFORMATION: **800-998-9938** • **707-829-0515** • **info@oreilly.com**